all color book of
RACING CARS
Brad King

Octopus
Octopus Books

Acknowledgements

The author and publishers would like to thank the following organizations and individuals for their help in supplying photographs for this book:

Alfa Romeo, Auto-Union (GB) Ltd, BP, Daimler Benz AG, Fiat, Mr C. Millar, Opel, Peugeot, Porsche, Régie Renault.

Stanbury Foley: 69 bottom; *Geoffrey Goddard:* 55 top; *Gero Hoschek:* 65, 72 bottom; *Gerold Kalt:* 71 top; *London Art Tech:* 18, 21 top, 41, 42, 44 top, 45 top, 46 top, 66 top, 67, 70 bottom, 71 bottom; *Roy Nockolds:* 9 (painting owned by Colin Crabbe), 11 (painting owned by Charles Noble, New York); *Peter Roberts Collection:* endpapers, title page, contents page, 4, 17, 19 top & bottom, 20 top, centre, bottom, 21 bottom, 22, 23 top & bottom, 24-25, 26 top & bottom, 27, 28, 29, 30 top & bottom, 31 top & bottom, 32 top & bottom, 33, 34 top, centre, bottom, 35, 36 top, centre, bottom, 37, 38 top & bottom, 39, 40 top & bottom, 43 top & bottom, 44-45 centre, 46 bottom, 47, 48 top, centre, bottom, 49, 50 top, centre, bottom, 51 top & bottom, 52 top, centre, bottom, 53, 54 top, centre, bottom, 55 bottom, 56-57, 58 top, centre, bottom, 59, 60 top & bottom, 61 top & bottom, 62 top, centre, bottom, 64 centre & bottom, 66 centre & bottom, 67 bottom, 68-69 top, 70 top & centre, 72 top; *Les Thacker:* 63 top & bottom.

First published in the United States of America
in 1973 by Crescent Books, a Division of Crown Publishers, Inc.,
419 Park Avenue South, New York, N.Y. 10016

ISBN 0 7064 0210 3

Produced by Mandarin Publishers Ltd.
77a Marble Road, North Point, Hong Kong.

Printed in Hong Kong.

Contents

Foreword

Motor racing has many classes, offering at one end of the scale vehicles and competitions suitable for amateur enthusiasts of modest means and, at the other, for professional teams employing the world's finest designers, engineers and drivers.

Formula One racing, or Grand Prix racing as it used to be called, is still the ultimate in motor sport, calling for the most advanced designs, the most sophisticated machinery and the highest skills in driving. So most of the cars pictured in this book, and mentioned in the introduction, are — or were — Formula One cars, although others are also shown, either because of special interest or for purposes of comparison.

Formula One 3 litre Ferrari.

Introduction

Breeding monsters

In the beginning there were no racing cars ... just cars, some of which were raced. That was how it was when the world's first motor race took place in 1895 from Paris to Bordeaux and back.

The event grew out of the previous year's Paris to Rouen Trial, sponsored by the Paris newspaper *Le Petit Journal*, and designed to improve the reliability of the horseless carriages of the day. This first motor sporting event soon developed into a free-for-all race (as soon as the starting officials were out of sight) which infected all the participants and some of those who watched it, with racing fever. Almost immediately, the Automobile Club de France was formed for the sponsoring of further contests.

After a procession across the pavé to Versailles, 22 cars set off on the 732-mile course. Competing were 15 petrol-engined cars, six steamers and one electric vehicle, but it was Emile Levassor who went to the front in his 1,200 c.c. 3½ h.p. Daimler-engined Panhard-Levassor.

At 3.30 next morning he reached Ruffec, 252 miles from the start, where he was due to hand over the tiller to his relief driver, but he was so far ahead of the estimated time of arrival that his co-driver was still sleeping, and rather than jeopardize the lead he had gained, Levassor carried on.

He reached Bordeaux at 10.40 a.m., nearly four hours ahead of his nearest rival, turned and set off on the return leg. When he reached Ruffec again his embarrassed co-driver was waiting, but Levassor was jealous by then, not only of his lead but of the fact that he had achieved it single-handed so he refused to hand over and carried on to the finish, which he reached nearly six hours before the next car, a Peugeot.

Levassor had been at the tiller of the solid-tyred car for an incredible 48 hours 48 minutes — his longest break 22 minutes — and had averaged nearly 15 m.p.h. Only seven other petrol-engined cars and a steamer finished the race.

His feat captured the imagination of motorists everywhere. Racing between Paris and other cities — in France at first, but later in other countries — soon became established as the major part of motor sport. Steamers, electrics and petrol-engined cars were all raced at first but it soon became apparent that petrol-engined cars were the most suited and that Panhards, for whom Levassor had evolved what was to become the conventional front-engined lay-out, were the most successful. Panhards were, in fact, the dominant marque during the first eight years of motor racing.

Inevitably, in the struggle to win races, cars grew bigger and more powerful. In 1898, although they still raced together, cars were divided into three classes — heavy, light and voiturette, or ultra-light, the idea of the voiturette class being to encourage less wealthy owners and to give them the chance of prizes in events which were almost certain to be won by the fortunate owners of Panhards or Mors. This was an aim which has continued to this day, though every new and inexpensive formula usually ends by being dominated by the competitors with the biggest resources.

Power rose, but not weight, for cars were stripped and had holes bored everywhere that holes could be bored to lighten them and increase the power to weight ratio.

In the 1895 Paris-Bordeaux-Paris race Levassor's Panhard had a 1.2 litre engine of 3½ h.p. and averaged 14.9 m.p.h. In 1899 the Canstatt-Daimler, one of the first cars designed for competition driving, had 5.5 litres and gave 25 h.p. The 1902 Paris-Vienna race was won by a 13.7 litre Panhard with nearly 90 b.h.p. at an average speed of 38.7 m.p.h.

Disaster became inevitable and it occurred in 1903 on the Paris-Madrid race, which was to become known as 'the race of death'. It was not just the rise in speed and the dangerous weakening of the cars in the search for lightness that were responsible; weekend crowds ignored all warnings and swarmed over the roads, and drivers were so blinded by the summer dust raised by other cars that at times some were steering only by glimpses of the tops of telegraph poles.

The death toll is uncertain, but it is believed that a score of competitors and spectators died before the French authorities halted the racers at Bordeaux and ordered the cars to be placed on trains and freighted back to Paris. After this, cars were generally separated in their classes to avoid mass-overtaking.

Racing was forced to move to circuits on closed roads, leading eventually to permanent circuits like Britain's Brooklands (opened in 1907) and America's Indianapolis (opened in 1911).

But cars still went on growing. By the time the French organized the first Grand Prix race on a circuit at Le Mans in 1906 specialized racing machines, longer, lower and higher-powered than production models, were essential to racing success. There was a maximum weight limit of 1,000 kg (19 cwt) for this race, but the Renault which won had an engine of 12.8 litres, developed 105 b.h.p. and averaged 62.88 m.p.h.

For the 1907 event at Dieppe, the weight restriction was abandoned in favour of a fuel consumption rule limiting cars to 30 litres per 100 km (9.4 m.p.g.). But Felice Nazzaro's winning Fiat was 15.26 litres and his speed was 70.61 m.p.h. Another car was close on 20 litres.

So in 1908 the Grand Prix authorities tried restricting the piston area. A four-cylinder engine was limited to 155 mm bore, a six-cylinder engine to 127 mm bore, but the result was that firms lengthened the stroke and Christian Lautenschlager won in a 12.8 litre Mercedes at 69 m.p.h.

The platinum tube burners of the earliest cars had been replaced by magneto ignition; mechanically operated inlet valves had been introduced and four-speed gearboxes had been introduced, yet revs were still comparatively low, of the order of 1,200 to 1,400 r.p.m. Brute power was all.

There was no Grand Prix in 1909, 1910 and 1911. Manufacturers held back because of the rising costs of racing and because the French manufacturers were sulking at the Mercedes victory, but at Daytona, USA, Barney Oldfield and Bob Burman raised records from 130 m.p.h. to 140 m.p.h. with the 21 litre Blitzen Benz.

In 1912 the French Grand Prix returned and was unrestricted apart from a minimum width requirement of 175 cm (68.5 inches). There were huge chain-driven Lorraine-Dietrichs of 15 litres capacity and Fiats of 14 litres, but the motoring world was in for a shock. The race was won by Georges Boillot in a Peugeot of only 7.6 litres. He averaged 68.45 m.p.h. and beat a Fiat of almost twice the Peugeot's size into second place.

A revolution had taken place. Its author was a 26-year-old Swiss named Ernest Henry who had produced for Peugeot an engine which revved at 2,200 r.p.m. It had four cylinders cast in one block including the cylinder head, and four valves per cylinder operated by twin overhead camshafts and the car had 100 m.p.h. performance. A milestone had been reached in motor racing. Brute power and size were no longer all important. Design efficiency was taking over.

In 1913 Peugeot confirmed their superiority. For this year there was a weight limit of 800 to 1,100 kg and a fuel consumption regulation of 20 litres per 100 km (14.1 m.p.g.). Boillot won again driving a new Henry-designed car of only 5.8 litres at an average of 72.13 m.p.h.

For 1914 there was introduced for the first time a restriction on engine capacity of the type generally followed in motor racing since. The limit was 4.5 litres; the 15 and 18 litre monsters were dead.

Peugeot were naturally the favourites and they had fully streamlined bodies and four-wheel brakes (as also had Fiats and Delages). But with the threat of war in the air, France was due for a humiliation. The five Mercedes cars had only two-wheel brakes but they had meticulously made engines with four valves and three plugs per cylinder, developed 115 b.h.p. at 2,800 r.p.m. and were capable of 110 m.p.h. And Mercedes brought something new to racing — team tactics and a strategic plan. Boillot drove well and led the race for most of the distance but he was pressured into blowing up his engine and Mercedes took the first three places.

A measure of the change that had taken place in six years was that when Lautenschlager had won the 1908 Grand Prix he had averaged 68.9 m.p.h. in a 12.8 litre car. On a more demanding course in 1914 he averaged 63.35 m.p.h. in a car barely more than a third of that capacity.

But then the war came and racing ceased. An era had ended just as a new age of sophistication had dawned.

Supercharged era

The litres shrank again when racing recommenced after the war; for 1921 the limit was 3 litres. Ernest Henry continued to influence design, having created eight-cylinder cars with twin overhead camshafts for Ballot, a French firm which made a brief but exciting foray into racing.

Ballots came second and third in the 1921 French Grand Prix, though the surprise winner was an eight-cylinder 115 b.h.p. Duesenberg, imported, with driver Jimmy Murphy, from the board tracks of America. Its notable feature was that it had hydraulic four-wheel braking, the brake fluid being water with glycerine added to prevent freezing.

In 1922 another new formula brought engines down to 2 litres. Fiat dominated at first with a six-cylinder car, which led Louis Coatalen to hire Bertarione from Fiat and Henry from Ballot to design six-cylinder models for Sunbeam. One of them, driven by Henry (later Sir Henry) Segrave won the 1923 French Grand Prix at Tours, the first Grand Prix victory for a British driver in a British racing car.

Meanwhile Fiat had been experimenting with supercharging. They were not the first to do so, but they were the first to win a Grand Prix with a supercharged car. Initially they used a Wittig vane-type blower which was not a success, but after they substituted a Roots type blower, Carlo Salamano won the European Grand Prix at Monza and the course of racing car design was changed.

Soon supercharging was widespread. In 1924 and 1925 Alfa Romeo dominated with the P2 designed by Vittorio Jano, another ex-Fiat man. It had a supercharged eight-cylinder engine giving 140 b.h.p. at 5,400 r.p.m. running on a blend of petrol and ethyl alcohol with a dash of ether.

Ettore Bugatti held out against supercharging. His Type 35, an eight-cylinder, three valves per cylinder, twin carburettor car was meticulously engineered and the first of his classic designs. But in 1926 even he was forced to capitulate and the use of superchargers became virtually universal.

The Italian born perfectionist of motor engineering gave way when a new formula brought down the litres again — to 1.5, making Grand Prix cars almost a voiturette class. The decision was taken because motor racing had been getting too expensive for the manufacturers and too fast for the authorities.

Under the new formula Bugatti cars duelled with the French Delage, designed by Albert Lory, which used a supercharged eight-cylinder engine with a complex train of more than 20 gears on roller bearings and gave 170 b.h.p. at 8,000 r.p.m.

Members of the public who preferred to watch more massive machines turned their eyes to Brooklands, where cars were grouped roughly by speed and they could see monsters like the Chitty-Chitty-Bang-Bangs, with World War One aero engines of 14 to 23 litres, driven by Count Louis Zborowski, and to Le Mans where, in the annual 24 hours race for catalogued sports and touring cars, started in 1923, there were the thundering creations of W. O. Bentley. Bentley cars won the race in 1927 and in the three following years, with the engine size growing from 3 to 6.5 litres. Though the race that was to be talked about most was the 1927 one, when Sammy Davis and 'Doc' Benjafield nursed 'Old Number 7' to victory after it was crippled in a multiple crash.

Grand Prix racing had become so restricted that inevitably the pendulum swung back. In 1928 the only restrictions were weight ones, and from 1930 the limits were off completely, and cubic capacity began to rise.

Riding mechanics had been barred since 1925 but cars had continued to have

Henry Segrave driving a 2 litre Sunbeam in the French Grand Prix at Strasbourg in 1922.

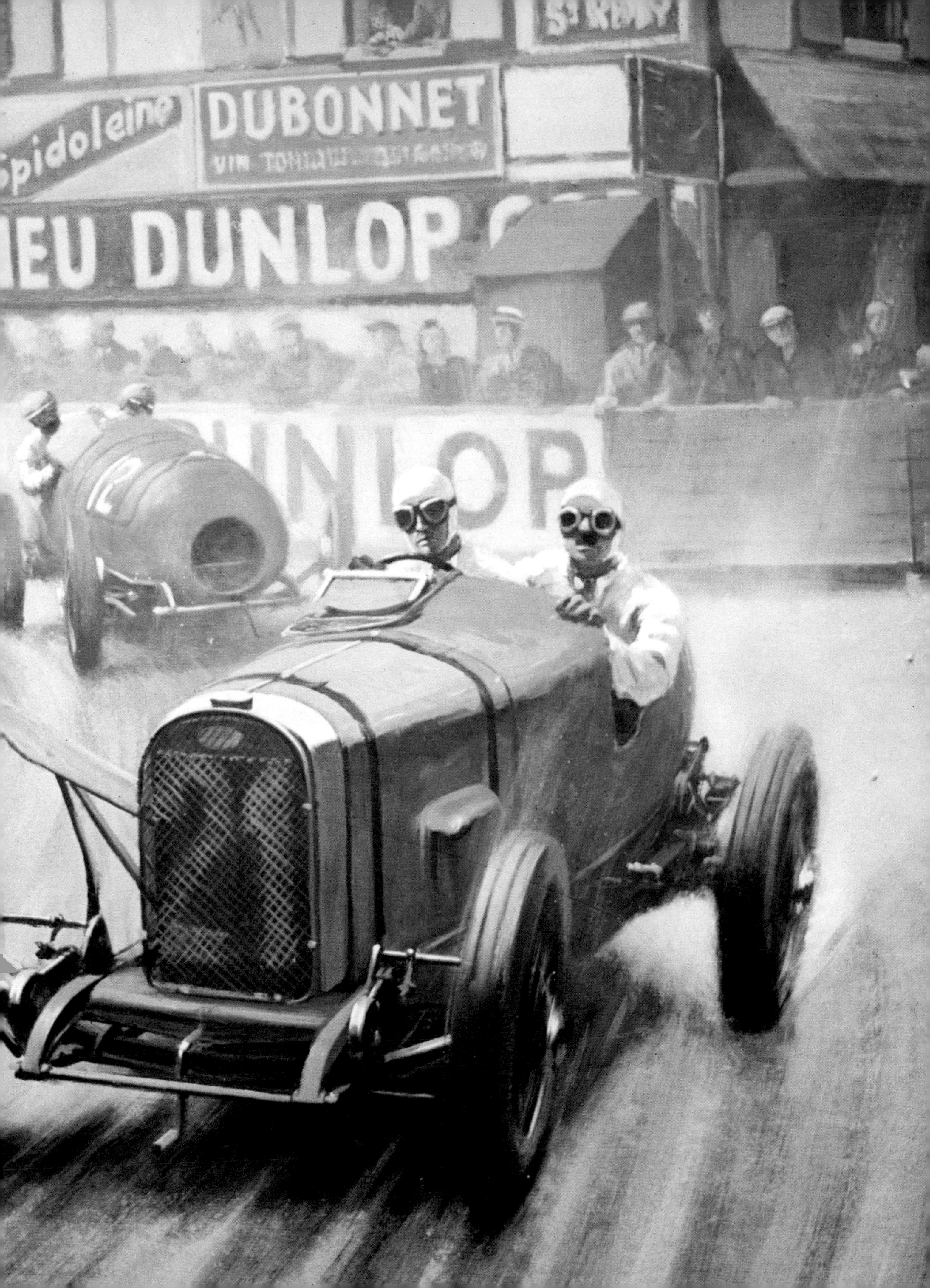
pidoleine
DUBONNET
VIN
EU DUNLOP
UNLOP
12

two-seat bodies until 1927, when single seaters were permitted. Alfa Romeo's P3 or Monoposto was the first successful genuine single seater. It had an unusual layout in that the differential was between the driver's legs and the propeller shaft was vee-shaped. The power rose from 2.9 to 3.2, then 3.8 litres; it was capable of over 140 m.p.h. and in the hands of Tazio Nuvolari and Rudolf Caracciola it was almost unbeatable.

Finally a new formula was agreed and introduced in 1934. It was known as the 750 formula because its chief restriction was that the weight of the car should not exceed 750 kg (1,653 lb). The authorities expected 2.5 litre cars to result from it, but what they were to get were 6 litre cars!

Nationalistic fervour was responsible. International prestige resulted from motor racing victories and Hitler wanted that prestige for Germany. He offered big subsidies to the makers of German cars that would vanquish those of other countries, and two rival German firms took on the brief. They were Mercedes-Benz and Auto-Union, a new company which was a consortium of four separate manufacturers, and it was Hitler's subsidies that encouraged their use of light alloys which allowed powerful engines despite the weight restrictions.

The Auto-Union P-Wagen was a revolutionary car. Ferdinand Porsche, who designed it, conceived the idea of placing the engine behind the driver to get the weight over the rear wheels. In this he anticipated general motor racing practice by two decades. The original engine was a V16 of 4.3 litres with a single supercharger at the rear. The car was fast, but the long tail and the concentration of weight at the rear made it a hard one for a driver to handle.

The rival Mercedes W25, designed by Hans Nibel and Max Wagner, was more conventional with a straight eight engine of 3.3 litres, which was soon increased to close on 4 litres, to give 430 b.h.p. at 5,800 r.p.m. Both cars had independent rear suspension.

The battle between the two makes was to set the tracks of Europe afire as the two teams established domination over other countries and fought for supremacy between themselves. Varzi, Stuck and Rosemeyer for Auto-Union, Caracciola, Fagioli and von Brauchitsch for Mercedes, were the heroes of all Germans and were watched with awe by men of other countries.

In 1935 Mercedes had the edge. In 1936 Auto-Union engines went up to 6 litres (520 b.h.p.) and Mercedes to 4.7 litres (495 b.h.p.). Auto-Union extended their wheelbases and Mercedes shortened theirs, and that was a mistake, and it was Auto-Union's year.

In 1937 Mercedes came back with the W125 with an eight-cylinder 5.6 litre engine giving 640 b.h.p. at 5,800 r.p.m. and a speed of nearly 200 m.p.h. The handling problems caused by the shortened wheelbase of the previous year had gone and it was probably the most powerful racing car ever built, though when the Auto-Union car went up to 6.1 litres the cars were on fairly equal terms.

The authorities became really alarmed and so for 1938 they clamped on a formula of 3 litres (or 4.5 unsupercharged, which was irrelevant since all the cars were blown) and a minimum weight of 850 kg. Auto-Union introduced a V12 giving 400 b.h.p. at 7,000 r.p.m., lengthened the nose and put the driver further back in the car to improve the handling. Mercedes matched them with a V12 of similar power.

Grand Prix competition had become a two-horse race. Manufacturers of other countries, unable to compete with the money of the German companies, began to turn their attention to voiturette events. In Italy, Alfa Romeo produced the Type 158, using a 1.5 litre eight-cylinder supercharged engine, which basically was half of their 16 cylinder Grand Prix engine. In Britain Raymond Mays and Peter Berthon evolved the ERA, a supercharged version of the six-cylinder 1.5 litre Riley.

These two cars were to have a big effect on motor racing, but the effect was to be delayed, for in 1939 Europe went to war again.

Dawn at Le Mans, 1929, Woolf Barnato driving a Bentley to victory.

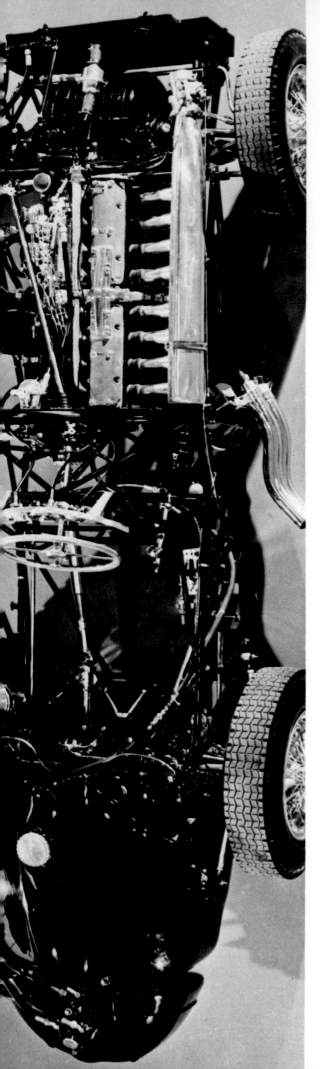

British supremacy

For the first post-war races the pre-war cars came out of mothballs. A new formula, introduced in 1947, limited engines to 1.5 litres supercharged or 4.5 litres unblown, and it was the pre-war Alfa Romeo 158, turning out 380 b.h.p. that dominated racing. When the World Championship for Drivers was introduced in 1950 the first winner was Giuseppe Farina, Italian leader of the Alfa Romeo team.

But supercharging was on the way out. Blowers were costly in fuel, which cost time for pit stops to refuel, and the endless quest for higher speeds from smaller engines created high internal stresses. Manufacturers began dreaming of unsophisticated, unstressed, unblown engines meeting the 4.5 litre limit.

Anthony Lago produced one in the Lago-Talbot, but it was Enzo Ferrari who was to give racing car design another change of course. Before the war Ferrari had operated the Scuderia Ferrari which acted as the racing department of Alfa Romeo. Now he engaged Aurelio Lampredi to design an unblown engine. The Ferrari that resulted made its debut at the Belgian Grand Prix of 1950, weighing in at 3.3 litres. Within months it had been bored out to the full 4.5 litres, giving 380 b.h.p. at 7,400 r.p.m. A tussle with the Alfas followed, but at the British Grand Prix at Silverstone in 1951 Ferrari saw his new car, driven by Gonzales, defeat the cars he used to run.

Britain's great hope, the supercharged BRM V16, built by the ERA team of Mays and Berthon with the backing of a score of patriotic firms and even the pennies of the public, was unreliable and Formula One racing developed into a Ferrari benefit.

There was so little competition for the Ferrari that the formula came to a premature end with World Championship events being run under the regulations for Formula Two, which had been introduced in 1948 for 2 litre unblown (or 500 c.c. supercharged) cars. In practice no one bothered with supercharging.

The result was still victory for Ferrari. Lampredi produced a 2 litre four-cylinder engine which gave 160 b.h.p. and this gave Alberto Ascari the Drivers' World Championship in 1952 and 1953. It was significant though that hard opposition came from a small British specialist firm. The Coopers, father and son, Charles and John, had entered motor racing making miniature 500 c.c. cars (powered by JAP speedway bike engines) which were the nursery for most of Britain's coming aces in the post-war period. In 1952 the Coopers put a 2 litre Bristol engine into a light body, and blond, bow-tied Mike Hawthorn gave the Ferraris such a battle in one that Ferrari signed Hawthorn for the following season.

In 1954 came a new Formula One of 2.5 litres without superchargers, or 750 c.c. blown, but supercharging was dead. The 2.5 formula was to be enormously popular. It lasted for seven years and it brought motor racing a mass following.

Mercedes-Benz made a return to the sport with a new car using fuel injection instead of carburettors, superb organization and teamwork. They also had the Argentine's Juan Manuel Fangio as their chief driver and he took the World Championship in 1954 and 1955.

But in 1955 Tony Brooks, unknown in Formula One racing, took a Connaught, the product of another small British specialist firm, to Syracuse and became the first Briton in a British car to win a Grand Prix for three decades. It was not an important Grand Prix and the Connaught firm was soon to fade away, but it was like a declaration of intent by Britain.

British cars had already achieved success in sports car racing. In the 24 hours Le Mans event C and D Type Jaguars of 3.4 to 3.8 litres were the winners in 1951 and 1953 (when they pioneered disc brakes), in 1955 (the year of motor racing's worst disaster when a Mercedes hit a Healey and more than 80 spectators died) and in 1956 and 1957.

In Formula One racing it was Fangio, 'Old Bandy Legs', rather than any constructor who dominated. He won the World Championship again in 1956 with a Lancia-Ferrari (Ferrari having taken over the Lancia racing cars) and in 1957 with the Maserati 250F.

In 1958, the year that alcohol fuel was outlawed, Fangio retired. Mike Hawthorn won the Drivers' World Championship in a Ferrari, but the Constructors' Championship was won by Britain's Vanwall, created by millionaire bearings manufacturer Tony Vandervell. He had been one of the original sponsors of the BRM but, after disagreements with other members of that unhappy project, he left to form his own team, his drivers being Stirling Moss, who missed the World Championship by a single point, Tony Brooks, the hero of Syracuse, and Stuart Lewis-Evans, tragically killed at the end of the season.

Suddenly cars in British racing green were packing the front rows of starting grids and the language of the pits seemed to have become English rather than Italian or Spanish.

The Vanwall stable disbanded in 1959 due to the illness of Tony Vandervell but Britain was now at the top. The World Championship was won by Australian Jack Brabham in a Cooper. This car used a 240 b.h.p. four-cylinder Coventry-Climax engine originally designed for fire pumps and it was sited where Cooper had sited the engine in their 500 c.c. midgets — behind the driver. And a new revolution now swept motor racing as every marque switched to rear-engined lay-outs.

Mobile hoardings

The year 1961 opened with a row. A new formula called for 1.5 litre unsupercharged engines. It also required the use of pump petrol and the fitting of self-starters, but it was the engine limit that caused the trouble. British manufacturers did not want the new formula. They claimed that there would be no spectacle or excitement with 1.5 litre cars and that Grand Prix cars must be bigger than this.

The British refused to believe that the new formula could be imposed against their wishes now that they were the main manufacturers of Formula One cars and therefore they made no plans to meet it. When it came in, despite their objections, they attempted to continue running 2.5 litre cars in a rival formula, but in the end they had to accept defeat and start catching up on wasted time.

Only one engine was available to them — a four-cylinder 1,475 c.c. Coventry-Climax unit that had first appeared in racing in Formula Two in 1957 — so Ferrari, who had begun early to prepare a V6 engine giving 180 b.h.p. at 9,000 r.p.m. had no difficulty in cleaning up, though it was remarkable that the World Champion driver was, for the first and only time, an American, Phil Hill.

But the following year it was Ferrari who was in trouble when many of his top technicians walked out after a dispute. And by this time British manufacturers had caught up. BRM, which was now part of the Owen Organization, had produced their own 1,498 c.c. V8 motor and the World Championship went to Londoner Graham Hill, though he had a battle throughout the season with Scotsman Jim Clark, driving the Coventry-Climax-engined Lotus created by Colin Chapman. In 1963 Clark took the title with a Lotus 25 fitted with the Mark Two version of the Coventry-Climax V8 engine, converted to fuel injection and giving 200 b.h.p. at 10,000 r.p.m.

The new formula had made it essential to save weight, and in order to do so and to maintain stiffness at the same time, Chapman had gone over to monocoque construction using a chassisless shell in place of the multi-tubular spaceframe. To fit within the new, low, slim body, Clark was required to adopt an almost prone position.

Other manufacturers followed this pattern and complaints were heard from enthusiasts about the 'sameness' of Formula One cars. Most were using the same Coventry-Climax engine and they also looked alike. Furthermore, with the drivers practically lying in their cars, they had almost disappeared from view. Only their helmeted heads showed above the cockpit. No longer could arms and elbows be seen working outside the car as they had a few years earlier, particularly when the driver was a big man, like Mike Hawthorn. The new cars were best suited to drivers built like jockeys. But the improvements in engines and in suspension and in tyres (which were growing bigger and wider) meant that 1.5 litre cars were soon lapping faster than 2.5 litre cars of five years earlier.

In 1964 the competition was very open and ended with Clark narrowly beaten for the title by John Surtees in a Ferrari V8. That year also saw the debut of Japan in Grand Prix racing. After dominating motor cycling with their high-revving, multi-cylinder machines, they had turned to four wheelers and produced the Honda V12 driven by American Ron Bucknum, but the 12 cylinder had teething troubles, and, indeed, Japan has still to make a mark in Grand Prix racing in the future.

There was also a debut in sports car racing in 1964. The Le Mans 24-hour event had been virtually a Ferrari monopoly since 1960. In 1964 Ford moved in for a confrontation. It was part of a vast programme to change the world-wide image of Ford from that of makers of 'tin lizzies' to makers of precision machinery, and towards this end they produced the GT40, a sports car so-called because it was only 40 inches high. Designed by Eric Broadley, who had created the Lola sports car, it used initially a 4.2 litre Indianapolis engine giving 350 b.h.p. at 7,200 r.p.m.

Ford also experienced teething troubles but they were to beat Ferrari in 1966 and dominate Le Mans for the next three years, by which time they had achieved what they had set out to do, and the appearance of the Le Mans car had changed from that of a production type of car to a mid-engined, power-packed, streamliner like something out of a science-fiction strip.

In the last year of the 1.5 litre Formula One in 1965, Clark and Lotus won again, and Clark even found time to jet to Indianapolis with a special Lotus to score the first British victory there.

The new Formula One introduced in 1966 provided for 3 litre engines and most manufacturers planned to use V12 engines. Naturally, problems were to be expected at first and full advantage of them was taken by the wily Jack Brabham, World Champion of 1959 and 1960, who had begun making his own Grand Prix cars four years earlier. He plumped for simplicity and reliability and used an Australian-made Repco V8 engine designed by Phil Irving. It gave only 285 b.h.p. at 8,200 r.p.m. but it was reliable and Brabham gave his car low weight and good handling. Brabham kept on going when cars with more sophisticated engines had stopped and the World Championship was his, the first time any driver had won it in a car of his own making. The following year Brabham surprised everyone again. This time Brabham's co-driver, Denny Hulme of New Zealand, took the title with Brabham second.

But it could not go on and it did not. In 1967 the Ford-backed Cosworth company produced a new V8 all-aluminium engine of 2,993 c.c. which gave 400 b.h.p. at 9,000 r.p.m. It was made available to all marques as the Coventry-Climax engine had been and most adopted it, but in 1968 it was Graham Hill who won in a Lotus-Ford 49B, after his team mate Jim Clark had been killed in a Formula Two race at Hockenheim in Germany.

Hill's winning Lotus was painted in red, white and gold and bore the words 'Players Gold Leaf Team Lotus' to advertise the tobacco company that were sponsoring the Lotus team. Traditional national colours had ceased to mean anything some years earlier when British marques began to dominate racing, and fuel and tyre companies had been backing teams for years, but the turning of a car into a mobile hoarding for a brand of cigarettes shocked many enthusiasts in Britain. However, advertising on cars was to spread.

So was the use of aerofoils — wings over the tail of a car to help keep it on the ground. They had been pioneered in sports car races by American Jim Hall's Chaparral cars in 1966, and Brabham and Ferrari introduced them to Formula One racing in 1968. In 1969 all cars sprouted them, but in the Spanish Grand Prix two Lotus cars had their aerofoils collapse and for the Monaco Grand Prix they were banned. But then the authorities relented and aerofoils were allowed, subject to limits on size, and have been with racing cars ever since.

The Ford Cosworth engine continued to power most contenders in Formula One. In 1969 Scotsman Jackie Stewart, driving a French Matra with the English Cosworth engine won the World Championship. Matra and McLaren and Lotus all experimented with four-wheel drive, which was not a new idea — Stirling

Moss had won a race in a four-wheel-drive experimental Ferguson car in 1961 — but the system was not found suitable in all conditions.

In 1970 came the debut of the March car, created, built (at Bicester, Oxford) and racing within a few months. Apart from running a works team March offered the car, which used the ubiquitous Cosworth engine, for general sale, and soon there were more March cars on the starting grid than any other marque.

One was bought for Jackie Stewart by his patron, timber merchant Ken Tyrrell, but the car failed to fulfil its early promise, and the World Championship was awarded posthumously for the first time. It went to Austrian driver Jochen Rindt, who had won four consecutive races in a Lotus 72 before his death during practice for the Italian Grand Prix at Monza. His points lead could not be overtaken.

However, Tyrrell had not intended relying on the March car alone and had ordered a car to be called the Tyrrell from Derek Gardner. It also used the Cosworth engine, which by 1971 was developing 450 b.h.p. and in that year Stewart won six Grands Prix and clinched the World Championship with it.

Tyrrell is one of the few private entrants left in Formula One racing, but equally the big car manufacturing companies have pulled out too. Today, cars are the products of small specialist firms, and are sponsored by companies which do not necessarily have any connection with motors or motoring. In 1972 the Surtees team was sponsored by a tea company, McLaren by a perfume company, BRM by cigarettes and Tecno by an aperitif. Lotus had ceased to use their name on their cars; they were simply John Player Specials.

But costs have risen astronomically. Levassor and his contemporaries were able to take ordinary road-going cars and race them. Today it costs something like a quarter of a million pounds to operate a Formula One team for a season. A prototype car costs around £25,000 to produce and later models may cost more than £8,000 each, and a team requires at least two cars and one spare. A Ford Cosworth engine costs £7,000 and the team needs six every year. Magnesium wheels cost £120 and tyres £35 each and a car may use 12 at a meeting.

Of course, this is life at the top. There are cheap racing categories in which novices can begin their drive to the front ranks. But all motor racing has changed since the days of Levassor's immortal drive in the first motor race in 1895. It has changed greatly even in the last quarter century. More power is being extracted from smaller engines and roadholding has improved. Drivers have changed too. Once they were well-to-do men who drove as a hobby; today's Formula One drivers are dedicated professionals, some with a high degree of engineering knowledge.

One thing has not changed however. Motor racing remains a dangerous sport; the death toll in recent years has been an appalling one, although new young stars emerge every year.

How will cars develop in the future? Turbo cars have been raced successfully, and the world land speed record is now held by a rocket-propelled vehicle. Motor development has never ceased, and it is never likely to do so.

CANSTATT-DAIMLER *(previous page)*
This was one of the first cars designed specially for competitive driving. It appeared in 1899, had a four-cylinder 5.5 litre engine developing 25 h.p. and was capable of a little over 50 m.p.h. A racing version of the Daimler Phoenix, it was built at the suggestion of Emil Jellinek, an Austrian driver who represented Daimler in Nice.

But with a short wheelbase and a high centre of gravity, the car was a dangerous one. Jellinek finished tenth and last in one in the 1900 Nice to Marseilles race and in the La Turbie hill climb at Nice the same year works driver Wilhelm Bauer died at the wheel when his car went wide on a bend.

Jellinek went to Canstatt. Daimler had just died, but Wilhelm Maybach, his long-time associate agreed to redesign the car, to make it longer, lower and more

powerful. He also agreed to change the name. The name proposed, and accepted, was that of Jellinek's 11-year-old daughter, Mercedes.

ROVER *(top right)* In the Isle of Man Tourist Trophy race of 1907 there were 22 starters but only two finishers. Winner of the six-lap, 240 mile race was a Rover 3.5 litre driven by E. Courtis. His speed was 28.8 m.p.h.

This compensated Rover for their misfortune the previous year when their entry had been excluded for late arrival.

HUMBER *(bottom left)* Tourist Trophy racing recommenced in the Isle of Man in 1914 after a five year lapse with a two-day, 600 mile race for cars of up to 3.3 litres.

Humber, who had supported racing for a decade at this time, produced this

twin overhead camshaft 3,288 c.c. car, which gave some 100 b.h.p. and a top speed of about 85 m.p.h.

Three cars were entered but were unsuccessful, the race being dominated by Sunbeam. Later, however, one of the cars won at Brooklands.

HUTTON *(bottom right)* It looked a Napier even to the water tower crowning the radiator. It was built at the Napier works in Acton, London, and, in fact, it was a Napier in everything but name.

It came into being because S. F. Edge, who exploited motor racing victories to sell Napier cars, wanted to enter a car for the 1908 TT race in the Isle of Man. Edge had so advertised the advantages of the Napier's six cylinders over four-cylinder cars that he dared not use the Napier name, and so he arranged to adopt the name of J. E. Hutton, a Surrey motor

distributor who had earlier made a small number of cars.

The Hutton had a four-cylinder 5,695 c.c. engine that was Napier-smooth and gave a speed of about 85 m.p.h. Three cars were built for the race and one driven by W. Watson won at 50.3 m.p.h. from two Darracqs, though the other Huttons — one driven by Hutton himself — failed to finish.

1902 FIAT CORSA *(top left)* The first Fiat car designed specially for competition driving, this was also the first of the marque with an all-steel chassis. The 24 h.p. four-cylinder engine of 6,371 c.c. gave it a top speed of nearly 60 m.p.h.

Vincenzo Lancia, the company's chief tester, drove it to win the Sassi-Superga hill climb in 1902 and it was later successful in a number of other hill climb events.

RENAULT GRAND PRIX *(centre left)* Louis Renault withdrew from racing after his brother Marcel was killed, but re-entered it in time for the first Grand Prix race, promoted by the French at Le Mans in 1906.

He entered three cars with 90 h.p. four-cylinder engines of 12,975 c.c. and the one driven by Hungary's Ferenc Szisz was the winner at 63 m.p.h. In 1907 Szisz came second to Nazzaro's Fiat.

But Renault ceased motor racing when the Grand Prix came to a temporary end in 1909 and the firm never re-entered it.

RENAULT PARIS-VIENNA *(bottom left)* Louis Renault's cars were distinguished by employing shaft-drive (instead of belts or chains) from the time of his first model in 1899. Then he used Aster and De Dion engines, but in 1902 he began making his own 3.7 litre four-cylinder engines.

For the 615 mile race from Paris to Vienna that year he entered three 16 h.p. machines in the light car class for vehicles of 400 to 650 kg, driving one of them himself.

But it was his brother Marcel who won both class and race, arriving in Vienna 45 minutes ahead of the first of the big cars, like Count Zborowski's 40 h.p. Mercedes. A year later Marcel died in the infamous Paris to Madrid race.

DE DIETRICH PARIS-MADRID *(top right)* The French firm of De Dietrich, which began making cars to the designs of Amédée Bollée, entered motor racing in 1899. For the Paris-Madrid race of 1903 they entered 10 cars of 30 h.p. 5.8 litres and 45 h.p. 9.8 litres.

The English driver Charles Jarrott was lying third in the race at 58.2 m.p.h. in one of the bigger cars when it was terminated at Bordeaux due to the number of fatal accidents that had occurred.

1913 OPEL *(bottom right)* A works team of two cars with four-cylinder 12 litre engines was entered for the French Grand Prix of 1913 but neither car finished. It was Peugeot's year.

In the following year the German firm produced an engine of 4,441 c.c. to comply with the 4.5 litre formula, but that year saw the triumph of the Mercedes.

FIAT S76 *(bottom left)* Bigger still was the Fiat S76, built in 1910, with a 28.3 litre engine from a dirigible, possibly the biggest four-cylinder engine ever used. Arthur Duray, an American-born Frenchman, covered a flying kilometre at Ostend at 132.37 m.p.h. in 1913, but this was not recognized as a world record since Duray made only a one-way run.

'BLITZEN' BENZ *(top right)* Benz also made a chain-driven monster, the 'Blitzen' or 'Lightning', which had a four-cylinder 21,504 c.c. engine developing 200 b.h.p. at 1,500 r.p.m. Victor Hemery covered a mile in 31.2 seconds, equal to a speed of about 120 m.p.h., in it in Brussels in 1909. Later in the year he lapped Brooklands at 127.88 m.p.h. to

set records that lasted until after World War I.

In America, Barney Oldfield acquired the Blitzen pictured, and reached 131.72 m.p.h. and in 1911 Bob Burman drove it at more than 140 m.p.h.

The car was mainly a record breaker and hill climber, but it also raced. L. G. 'Cupid' Hornsted took 27 world records with a Blitzen but also drove it to victory in three races at Ostend in 1914, and a Blitzen was still being raced in England by Sir Alistair Miller as late as 1930.

MERCEDES GRAND PRIX *(bottom right)* The French Grand Prix of 1914 was the first to be run under an engine-size restriction of the type used ever since – 4.5 litres in this case. It was also

the race in which team tactics were used to win for the first time.

Mercedes came to the race with immaculately prepared new cars and with a pre-planned strategy. Georges Boillot in a Peugeot was the favourite for he had won the race the previous year, but the Mercedes drivers, working to pre-race instructions, expended one of their cars in pressuring him until he blew his Peugeot up, and then came in first, second and third, Christian Lautenschlager, the winner, averaging 63.35 m.p.h.

The Mercedes cars had four-cylinder engines of 4,483 c.c. developing 115 b.h.p. and capable of more than 100 m.p.h.

FIAT 'MEPHISTOPHELES' *(previous page)* Typifying the massive litreage of racing's early era was the Fiat 'Mephistopheles' with its 18,155 c.c. engine. In 1908, a year after the opening of Brooklands, the world's first permanent racing circuit, when the promoters were casting around for crowd-pulling attractions, 'Mephistopheles' was brought to Britain to be matched against the 20 litre Napier 'Samson' of S. F. Edge.

The Napier led for the first three of the six laps but then a crankshaft failed and Felice Nazzaro, the Fiat ace, had no more competition. 'Mephistopheles' was reputed to have lapped at over 120 m.p.h. and went on racing at Brooklands until 1922, when the mighty engine blew up. It was rebuilt and modified by Ernest Eldridge and broke the world speed record in 1924 at 146.01 m.p.h.

FIAT S74 *(top left)* Virtually the last of the chain-driven racing giants, the Fiat S74 had a four-cylinder 14.13 litre engine giving 140 b.h.p. at 1,700 r.p.m. After the Lorraine-Dietrich, which had an engine of over 15 litres, it was the biggest car in the 1912 French Grand Prix.

Three ran and they were the fastest cars in the race, the American driver David Bruce-Brown being timed at over 101 m.p.h. before he retired. But this race saw the triumph of Georges Boillot and the revolutionary 7.6 litre Peugeot. Fiat had to be content with second place, won by Louis Wagner at 67.32 m.p.h.

FIAT S57 *(bottom left)* Fiat did not compete in the 1913 French Grand Prix, but for the 4.5 litre formula of 1914 it built three cars with four-cylinder 130 b.h.p. engines. They carried side-mounted spare wheels, had pointed tails and pioneering four-wheel brakes, but 1914 was the year of Mercedes.

During the war the engines were enlarged to 4.9 litres and the power raised to 150 b.h.p. for Indianapolis. They never got there, but Count Giulio Masetti won the Targa Florio with one in 1921.

VAUXHALL 30/98 *(previous page)*
A Stockport textile manufacturer named Joseph Higginson went to Vauxhall designer Laurence Pomeroy in March 1913 and explained that he was set on capturing the Shelsley Walsh hill climb record at the June meeting.

With no time to design a new car, Pomeroy enlarged the four-cylinder engine of the Prince Henry sports car to 4.5 litres, fitted it in a four-seater doorless body and called it the 30/98 (the figures having no particular meaning).

Higginson set a new record which stood for 15 years. Pomeroy made another 30/98 and within a year the two cars had won 18 first places and the same number of second places in a variety of events.

Production of the 100 b.h.p. car began just after the start of World War I. With a guarantee that 'It will attain 100 m.p.h. on the track,' it became one of the greatest of vintage cars and production went on into the late twenties.

This picture shows the 1927 model.

DELAGE 5.1 litre *(bottom left)*
Concentrating on short sprint and hill climb events in the early twenties, the French firm of Delage produced this six-cylinder 5,136 c.c. o.h.v. engined car capable of 120 m.p.h. French driver René Thomas broke records at Mont Ventoux in 1922 and La Turbie in 1923, after which the car was imported to Britain by Captain (later Sir) Alistair Miller to race at Brooklands.

It became known as Delage I to distinguish it from its bigger sister, Delage II, a six-litre model built in 1925 which also recorded the fastest times of the day at Mont Ventoux and La Turbie and was also imported to England.

BENTLEY 4.5 litre *(right)* Few cars are remembered with so much affection and admiration as this hero of Le Mans and Brooklands. A single car made its Le Mans debut in 1927 but was wrecked in the multiple crash at the White House. That year the race was won by a 3 litre Bentley. In 1928 the 4.5 litre car won at 69.11 m.p.h.

Most distinguished of the breed was the supercharged model driven by Sir Henry 'Tim' Birkin, who continued racing it after the disbanding of the Bentley team in 1930. Fitted with a single-seat body and a pointed tail, it raised the Brooklands lap record to 137.96 m.p.h. in 1931 and was driven by Birkin until his death in 1933.

The car had a 4,398 c.c. engine which originally gave 110 b.h.p. but later, with a Villiers supercharger, this figure was more than doubled.

SALMSON *(top left)* Originally engaged in making aero engines, the French Salmson company ran a successful voiturette team in the twenties. With a four-cylinder twin overhead camshaft engine of 1,087 c.c. the Salmson was capable of well over 100 m.p.h. in supercharged form.

Designer Emil Petit created an eight-cylinder model using two superchargers in 1927 but this was less successful.

BUGATTI Type 35B *(bottom left)* More than 2,000 awards were won by cars of Bugatti's Type 35 range; they were the most numerous and most successful Grand Prix cars of the late twenties. In fact there were Bugatti-only races. The precision of their workmanship was famed; so was their roadholding.

The range, which included 1.5 and 2 litre models, was begun in 1924. The 35B was launched in 1927 with a 2,270 c.c. single o.h.c. eight-cylinder engine with a supercharger on the offside. It won Grands Prix everywhere until its replacement by the more powerful Type 51 in 1931.

BUGATTI Type 13 BRESCIA *(top right)* First of Ettore Bugatti's distinguished designs, this small, light car took a decade to win its popular name. Production began at Molsheim, near Strasbourg in 1910 with a 1,327 c.c. engine. The next year the capacity was increased to 1,368 c.c. and in the French Grand Prix Ernst Friderich came second to a 10 litre Fiat, but there were few events suitable for voiturettes.

World War I came and the car was mothballed. When racing restarted Friderich took it out again and in 1921 he won the voiturette class of the first Italian Grand Prix at Brescia at 72 m.p.h. and was followed home by a string of other Bugattis. And that was how the car acquired the name Brescia.

FIAT 804 *(bottom right)* Designed for the two-litre Grand Prix formula which began in 1922, this car ran in only two races, and yet it was a trendsetter. Its chassis was tapered in with the body at the rear and this feature was to be much copied. The engine was a six-cylinder of 1,991 c.c. giving 92 b.h.p. at 4,500 r.p.m.

Three cars were entered for the 1922 French Grand Prix at Strasbourg, the event which introduced the mass start. Two of the cars failed but Felice Nazzaro won the 500-mile race at 79 m.p.h. finishing nearly an hour ahead of the field.

Power was increased for the Italian Grand Prix at Monza and several teams dropped out as soon as Fiat entered. In fact the cars came first and second, but were then succeeded by the 805, which established the supercharger in Grand Prix racing.

FIAT 806 *(top left)* Only one car was built and only one race was entered with it, though it had a phenomenal victory. The Fiat 806 was designed for the 1.5 litre Grand Prix formula and had a triple o.h.c. 12-cylinder, 24 valve engine of 1,493 c.c. which turned out a remarkable 175 b.h.p. at 7,500 r.p.m.

Pietro Bordino, Fiat's Italian works driver, drove the car in the 1927 Milan Grand Prix, which was run as a Formula Libre event, and beat bigger engined Alfa Romeos and Bugattis on a wet track to win at 94.58 m.p.h.

Three cars were to have been entered for further races but it never happened; the directors took Fiat out of Grand Prix racing and Bordino switched to driving a Bugatti 35B.

ALFA ROMEO P2 *(bottom left)* Alfa's first Grand Prix car, the P1 of 1923, was never raced. Ugo Sivocci, its driver, was killed in practice for the debut. Its successor, designed by Vittorio Jano, made its appearance the following year with a supercharged eight-cylinder 1,987 c.c. engine turning out 155 b.h.p. at 5,500 r.p.m.

It won the French Grand Prix and then took first, second and third places in the Italian Grand Prix, with Antonio Ascari setting a new Monza lap record of 104.24 m.p.h. which lasted for six years.

In 1925 the car won the Belgian and Italian Grands Prix and was leading in the French at Montlhéry when Ascari left the road in drizzling rain and was killed. But the P2 was the car of the year and Alfa added a laurel wreath to their badge.

The arrival of a new formula in 1926 caused the withdrawal of the P2, though it was to reappear in Formula Libre events and was still raced with success by Scuderia Ferrari as late as 1930.

thirties

ALFA ROMEO 8C-2300 *(previous page)*
This type got its name because it made
its Grand Prix debut in the 1931 Italian
Grand Prix at Monza and took first and
second places. But the car was designed
originally by Vittorio Jano as a sports car
and had two-seat bodywork. As a sports
car it was used by Lord Howe and Sir
Henry Birkin to win Le Mans and by
Nuvolari to win the Targa Florio.

Originally the car had a 2,336 c.c.
eight-cylinder engine with a Roots type
supercharger developing some 150 b.h.p.
at more than 5,000 r.p.m. and a top
speed of about 130 m.p.h. Enzo Ferrari,
whose Scuderia Ferrari constituted the
Alfa racing department at this time, later
increased the capacity to 2.6 litres (as in
the car pictured) and it ran in the Mille
Miglia of 1934 and 1935 but by then it
was no longer a match for the Maseratis
and Bugattis.

The Type B Monoposto (or P3) was derived from it and succeeded it in Grand Prix events.

LAGONDA 4.5 litre *(top left)* The British car firm assailed sports car racing in 1934 with the Rapide, which used a six-cylinder 4,453 c.c. push-rod o.h.v. engine. It gained placings in the Tourist Trophy race that year and in 1935, but its greatest success came in the 1935 Le Mans 24 hours race.

Since the last Bentley victory in 1930 the race had gone every year to Alfa Romeo, but J. S. Hindmarsh and Louis Fontes drove the Lagonda to win at 77.85 m.p.h. There were more placings at Brooklands and other tracks in the following years.

PEUGEOT 301C *(centre left)* This four-cylinder 1,467 c.c. engined sports car broke the Class F 24-hour record at Miramas, near Marseilles, in 1932, covering more than 1,646 miles and averaging more than 68 m.p.h.

It was driven by André Boillot, younger brother of the 1913 French Grand Prix winner. He died shortly afterwards while testing a Peugeot sports car.

PEUGEOT DARL'MAT *(bottom left)* Emile Darl'Mat developed this racing two-seater sports car from the aerodynamic Peugeot 402 saloon which was introduced in 1936. Three of his sports cars with their modified 2 litre o.h.v. engines ran in the 1937 Le Mans 24 hours race and finished in seventh, eighth and tenth places (second, third and fifth in the 2 litre class).

After this Darl'Mat cars went on sale to the public at just under £500, but

World War II prevented further development of the marque.

ALFA ROMEO P3 *(bottom right)* Also known as the Type B or simply as 'the Monoposto', because it was the first successful single-seater, the Jano-designed P3 used an engine from the Monza, first bored out to 2.65 litres and enlarged successively to 2.9 then 3.2 and finally to 3.8 litres.

With the eight-cylinder double-supercharged engine developing 190 b.h.p. at 5,400 r.p.m., and low body weight, the car won its first grande épreuve, the Italian Grand Prix of 1932, and was beaten only twice in its first season.

MASERATI 1.5 litre *(top left)* No one could compete on equal terms with the State-sponsored German Grand Prix teams in the second half of the thirties and the Italians decided to concentrate on voiturette racing.

Maserati produced a supercharged six-cylinder twin o.h.c. engine of 1,493 c.c. giving 155 b.h.p. at 6,200 r.p.m. and the 6CM figured in great numbers in Italian events, giving Luigi Villoresi several successes between 1936 and 1938.

Then, with the competition of the Alfa Romeo 158, Maserati switched to a supercharged four-cylinder engine of 1,496 c.c., the 4CM, in the same chassis, but it could not equal the 'Alfette'.

ERA *(centre left)* Raymond Mays and Peter Berthon, with the financial backing of Humphrey Cook, produced the first ERA (for English Racing Automobile) in 1934 to fight the Continentals in the 1.5 litre voiturette class. Using Riley-based, six-cylinder supercharged engines ERA swept the board and 1.1 and 2 litre variants followed.

Most famous of the cars was Romulus, a B type with the 1,488 c.c. engine developing 150 b.h.p. at 6,500 r.p.m. which was bought by Prince Chula of Siam as a twenty-first birthday present for his cousin Prince Birabongse. Driving under the name 'B. Bira' the young prince recorded 10 first and 13 placings in 30 starts between 1936 and 1939.

Raymond Mays' own 2 litre car was outstanding in hill climbs and the ERA was the most successful marque of 1937, continuing on the racing circuits for many years more. It led directly to the post-war BRM.

AUTO UNION C Type *(bottom left)* Auto Union's answer to the awe-inspiring Mercedes-Benz W125 in 1937 had a rear-mounted 6.1 litre V16 engine giving 520 b.h.p. The team's star driver, Bernd Rosemeyer won the Eifel, Pescara and Donington Grands Prix and also the Vanderbilt Cup in America before meeting his death in January 1938 in a record-breaking attempt.

His team mates managed two other victories — in Belgium and South Africa — but in the last year of the 750 kg formula the 22 cwt Auto Union did not equal the Mercedes-Benz in either reliability or handling.

DERBY-MASERATI *(right)* The French firm of Derby had considerable success with voiturette racing cars in the early thirties, particularly when they were driven by Mrs. Gwenda Stewart: a pioneer woman racer who set records at Montlhéry and Brooklands.

The Derby-Maserati was introduced in 1935 and was a front-wheel-drive single-seater with a four-cylinder Maserati 1,496 c.c. engine mounted back to front. The car had all-independent suspension by means of swinging arms and leaf springs and 125 m.p.h. top speed.

MERCEDES-BENZ W154 *(top left)* This was the Mercedes entry for the 3 litre formula which began in 1938. It had a 2,960 c.c. supercharged V12 engine giving nearly 450 b.h.p. at 8,000 r.p.m. and it won five races in the first season and established supremacy over the Auto Unions.

In 1939 the car won again, but there was tragedy in the Belgian Grand Prix when the British driver Dick Seaman, rising star of the Mercedes team, crashed into a tree and his 154 burst into flames. He died in hospital while his team mate Hermann Lang won the race in a similar car.

MERCEDES-BENZ W125 *(bottom left)* This was the most powerful Grand Prix car ever built. The eight-cylinder

supercharged engine of 1936 had been enlarged to 5.6 litres to give a fearsome 640 b.h.p. at 5,800 r.p.m. and a speed of nearly 200 m.p.h. To obtain better road holding, the chassis had been lengthened and independent rear suspension had been abandoned in favour of a return to the de Dion axle used at the turn of the century. This consisted of jointed half-shafts to each wheel, with the wheels linked by a floating tube.

The W125 dominated the last season of racing under the 750 kg maximum weight formula. Hermann Lang, Rudolf Caracciola and Manfred von Brauchitsch cleaned up the major events between them, winning the Tripoli, German, Monaco, Swiss, Masaryk and Italian Grands Prix.

But the authorities were alarmed at

the power struggle, and for 1938 there was a new formula which limited supercharged cars to 3 litres.

MERCEDES-BENZ W165 *(right)* Italy decided to run the 1939 Tripoli Grand Prix as a voiturette race to rule out the Germans, but they received a shock. Mercedes scaled down the 154 and put in a 1,493 c.c. supercharged V8 engine developing 273 b.h.p. at 7,800 r.p.m.

Hermann Lang won the race at 122.91 m.p.h. with Rudolf Caracciola in another W165 in second place. Mercedes had demonstrated that they could dominate the 1.5 litre league as easily as the 3 litre if they chose, but they did not choose, and the W165 had run its one and only race.

ALFA ROMEO 159 *(top left)* For 1951 the 158 was modified and improved to give 385 b.h.p. at 9,500 r.p.m. and renamed the 159. It brought Juan Manuel Fangio his first World Championship. Yet it was Alfa's last Grand Prix car.

ALFA ROMEO 158 *(bottom left)* This astonishing small car was to win a World Championship 13 years after its debut in 1938. The Type 158, designed by Gioacchino Colombo, used half of the V16 Grand Prix engine in a scaled down Grand Prix car. The supercharged 1,479 c.c. eight-cylinder twin o.h.c. unit gave nearly 200 b.h.p. at 7,500 r.p.m. and the 'Alfette' was only beaten once in the last season before the war.

After the war the car returned in Formula Libre events and when the 1.5 supercharged Formula One was introduced in 1947, it became a Grand Prix car. The power was raised to 250 b.h.p. and later to 265 b.h.p., and the veteran car was *still* virtually unbeatable.

In 1950 Giuseppe Farina, Luigi Fagioli and Reg Parnell came first, second and third in the European Grand Prix at Silverstone, and Farina became the first to win the title of World Champion, introduced that year.

FIFTIES

CONNAUGHT Type B SYRACUSE

(previous page) Tony Brooks was an unknown dentist and inexperienced racing driver in 1955. He had never raced a Formula One car and never raced abroad. And then, squeezing into the cockpit of a Connaught for the first time, he roared through the 240-mile Syracuse Grand Prix to beat Luigi Musso's Maserati, to break the lap record and give Britain its first Grand Prix win for three decades.

The car was the product of a small concern run by Rodney Clarke on the Portsmouth road at Send in Surrey. The car used a 2,470 c.c. four-cylinder Alta engine giving 250 b.h.p. at 6,500 r.p.m. in a tail-finned aerodynamic body. It had been developed the year before on a pathetically small budget.

For Brooks the victory meant the start of a career. He was signed by BRM and later by Vanwall and Ferrari. For Connaught it did remarkably little. By 1957 the budget would stretch no further and the firm was sold.

MERCEDES-BENZ W196 *(bottom left)*

The silver arrows of Mercedes-Benz flashed back into Grand Prix racing in 1954, backed by a 500-strong team of engineers and factory staff. Even their transporters were capable of 100 m.p.h. and the W196 was worthy of this lavish treatment.

It had a straight-eight engine of 2,496 c.c. with fuel injection and desmodromic valve gear, and it achieved 290 b.h.p. at 8,700 r.p.m. In 1954 Fangio drove it to win the Grands Prix of France, Germany, Switzerland and Italy and became World Champion. In 1955 he was joined by Stirling Moss and they were beaten only once, Fangio becoming World Champion again. Then, with their conquest complete, Mercedes packed away their cars and retired from Formula One racing.

JAGUAR D-Type *(top right)* For three

years the two-seater D-Type was unbeatable in the Le Mans 24-hours race. With a six-cylinder 3,442 c.c. engine giving 250 b.h.p. at 5,750 r.p.m., it made its Le Mans debut in 1954, averaging 105 m.p.h. for 24 hours on a streaming wet track in the hands of Tony Rolt and Duncan Hamilton, and being only narrowly beaten by the more brutal 4.9 litre Ferrari.

The following year, despite motor racing's worst disaster, Mike Hawthorn and Ivor Bueb won at Le Mans at 107 m.p.h. Smooth and aerodynamic, the car triumphed again in 1956 and 1957, by which time it had a 3.7 litre engine, and production models were available at £3,878. The D-type's last appearance at Le Mans was in 1960.

HWM *(bottom right)* They had only a

shoestring budget, but John Heath and George Abecassis created Britain's first successful post-war works team. The name HWM stood for Hersham and Walton Motors, which was the garage they ran, and the prototype of their racing car was a 2 litre Alta which Heath rebuilt in 1948. It was a two-seater which doubled as a sports car and a Formula Two car.

For 1950 HWM used the four-cylinder 1,960 c.c. Alta engine (the only real racing engine available) which gave about 125 b.h.p. and a top speed of about 130 m.p.h. The cars still had two-seat bodies, though they ran only in monoposto events, but for 1951 they had single-seat bodies.

One of the team drivers was a young Stirling Moss, who won half a dozen placings during 1951 and 1952. But in 1953 the cars were outclassed, even though the final version claimed more than 175 b.h.p. HWM turned to sports car racing with Jaguar-engined cars, but Heath lost his life in one in the 1956 Mille Miglia and the firm's racing came to an end.

VANWALL *(top left)* Tony Vandervell, millionaire boss of a bearings company, entered motor racing as one of the backers of the BRM project, but withdrew in 1951. He then bought a 4½ litre Ferrari as a high-speed test bed and started his own racing stable, calling his modified Ferrari the Thinwall Special.

The first Vanwall Special followed in 1954, a single car with a 2 litre four-cylinder engine designed by Leo Kusmicki, an ex-Norton motorcycle engineer. Basically it was four 500 c.c. Norton engines in one package.

In 1956 came the Vanwall proper. Frank Costin and Colin Chapman designed a new frame, low-drag body and suspension system. The engine had grown to 2,490 c.c. with Bosch fuel injection, developing 280 b.h.p. at 7,400 r.p.m. With it Stirling Moss won the 1956 International Trophy race at Silverstone at 100.47 m.p.h. and the 1957 British Grand Prix at Aintree.

The year 1958 saw Vandervell's triumph. For the first time British cars dominated Formula One racing. Moss

won the Dutch, Portuguese and Moroccan Grands Prix, Tony Brooks won the Belgian, German and Italian, and the Vanwall beat Ferrari to win the Manufacturers' Championship.

BRM 2.5 litre FORMULA 1 *(top right)* After the over-sophistication and complexity of the original BRM the car for the 2.5 litre formula which began in 1955 was refreshingly simple. The aim was the basic one of fitting a high-powered four-cylinder engine into a lightweight body. In fact, the 2,497 c.c. engine delivered some 270 b.h.p. at 7,500 r.p.m.

Yet a great number of drivers were to pilot the BRM, and Mike Hawthorn and Tony Brooks were to experience crashes, before Jean Behra and Harry Schell began to achieve some success with it in 1957.

And it was 1959 before Sweden's Joakim Bonnier steered the car to its first victory in a World Championship event at Zandvoort in Holland.

The six-cylinder 2.49 litre car, which provided some 260 b.h.p. at 7,600 r.p.m., was the main choice of private entrants during the life of the 2.5 litre Formula One. But at the end of 1957 Maserati were forced to withdraw from racing for financial reasons.

LOTUS 2.5 litre FORMULA 1
(left) Colin Chapman's company entered Formula One racing in 1958 after success with sports cars. The first Grand Prix car, driven by Graham Hill, used the Coventry Climax 2.5 litre four-cylinder engine front-mounted in a small-diameter tubular frame, with the body of the car built up at the rear.

But the car was prone to breakage in its first two years and no match for the Cooper driven by Jack Brabham. Lotus had to wait until 1960 for its first win by Stirling Moss in a car entered by Rob Walker, in which he averaged 67.4 m.p.h. at Monaco.

MASERATI 250F *(above centre)* An unsophisticated car but a light and attractively designed one that was always a potential winner in the hands of a good driver – as Juan Manuel Fangio proved when he won the Argentine and Belgian Grands Prix with the brand new car in 1954, before he moved to Mercedes-Benz.

Stirling Moss took over the Maserati leadership and was runner-up to Fangio in the World Championship in 1955 and 1956. Then in 1957 Fangio returned to Maserati and won the Argentine, Monaco, French and German Grands Prix to gain his fourth successive World Championship and give Maserati their first.

COOPER-BRISTOL 2 litre *(above right)* Formula One racing was in the doldrums in 1952 and Formula Two became the premier class. The Cooper-Bristol was the best of the British 2 litre cars. It was very light at 9¼ cwt, and the six-cylinder 1,971 c.c. engine gave 150 b.h.p. at 5,750 r.p.m. Mike Hawthorn was its outstanding driver, winning many races, which got him a job as a Ferrari driver in 1953.

The Cooper-Bristol had little more success in Formula Two, but Hawthorn's car was rebuilt in 1953 as a sports car with full-width bodywork and Alan Brown won a number of races with it.

LANCIA-FERRARI *(top left)* Lancia's D50 Grand Prix car made its debut in 1954 and was raced with some success by Alberto Ascari, but the next year Ascari was killed in a sports car crash at Monza and simultaneously the Lancia firm experienced financial pressures. They sold their racing cars and spares to Enzo Ferrari as the man best suited to maintain Italian prestige on the circuits, and he renamed them Lancia-Ferraris.

The cars had a 2,487 c.c. V8 engine giving about 250 b.h.p. at 8,200 r.p.m. Ferrari had acquired Fangio from Mercedes-Benz as his leading driver and the Argentinian (pictured at the wheel) won four grandes épreuves and the World Championship title in 1956.

By 1957 Ferrari had modified the engine, chassis and suspension of the cars considerably. He had also lost Fangio to Maserati. The season was a failure, and at the end of it the Lancia-Ferraris were broken up and Ferrari introduced his V6 Dino model.

MASERATI 300S *(bottom left)* Based on the 250F Grand Prix car, the 300S sports car used a 2,991 c.c. engine giving 250 b.h.p. at 6,500 r.p.m. It made its debut at Sebring in 1955 and raced to the end of 1957. Jean Behra, Luigi Musso and Stirling Moss all drove it with success but the car was never equal to the Mercedes 300 SLR or the Jaguar D-Type.

SIXTIES

PORSCHE 1.5 litre FORMULA 1
(previous page) The air-cooled
horizontally-opposed flat-eight engine of
1,494 c.c. used by Porsche for their 1961
debut in Formula One racing was less
powerful than the engines of their British
rivals, giving only some 180 b.h.p. at
9,250 r.p.m.

But Dan Gurney and Jo Bonnier left
BRM to drive the tubular chassis Porsche
and Gurney won the French Grand Prix
of 1962. However, this was to be
Porsche's only grande épreuve victory and
they decided they were more at home
with sports car racing and withdrew from
the Formula One scene.

LOLA-CLIMAX 1.5 FORMULA 1 *(top
left)* Eric Broadley had made his name
with Lola sports cars, which took their
name from the pop song, 'Whatever Lola
wants'. In 1962 Bowmaker sponsored a
team of four Formula One Lolas. The

design was based on a Formula Junior car and the engine inevitably was the Coventry-Climax V8.

John Surtees, former world motor-cycle racing champion, who had just turned full-time to cars, won a race at Mallory Park and had several placings, but the team disbanded at the end of the year.

However, Surtees had made an impression on Ferrari, who signed him to drive the following year.

BRM 1.5 FORMULA 1 *(centre left)* BRM were also forced to rely on the Coventry-Climax engine at the start of the 1.5 litre Formula One, but they worked rapidly to build their own and in 1962 came the BRM Type 56 with 1,498 c.c. engine, which was to give Graham Hill victory in four grandes épreuves and the World Championship.

BRM, so long tagged as an 'unlucky' stable, had finally lived down the memories of their earlier disappointments.

For 1963 they had a new six-speed gearbox and a duralumin semi-monocoque designed by Tony Rudd and, though the World Championship eluded them, Hill was runner-up in that year and the following two.

LOTUS-CLIMAX 1.5 FORMULA 1 *(bottom left)* Colin Chapman revolutionized Formula One racing car bodies with his Mark 25 which made its debut in 1962. He pioneered a riveted box monocoque type of construction, more rigid than the conventional tubular space frame. It was to be widely copied.

A year later the Coventry-Climax V8 engine was converted to fuel injection to give 200 b.h.p. and Jim Clark scored seven victories in grandes épreuves, plus another five in other Formula One races, and became World Champion. The

picture shows him winning the British Grand Prix at Silverstone.

HONDA 1.5 FORMULA 1 *(bottom right)* After changing motorcycle racing beyond recognition, the Japanese firm of Honda moved into Formula One motor racing in 1964 with an experimental monocoque with a V12 engine in a tubular rear subframe. The 1,495 c.c. with Honda fuel injection was designed to give 230 b.h.p. at a startling 12,000 r.p.m. The car was driven by American sports car driver Ron Bucknum, joined a year later by fellow countryman Richie Ginther.

Inevitably there were teething troubles, for the Japanese had no motor racing background and, in fact, the car's first success came in the last 1.5 litre Grand Prix when Richie Ginther won in Mexico City.

COOPER-CLIMAX 1.5 FORMULA 1
(top) British cars had to rely on the
same Coventry-Climax 1,498 c.c. V8
engine, giving 200 b.h.p. at 10,000 r.p.m.
at the start of the 1.5 litre formula.
Cooper were the first to receive one but
there was no time to get the car and
engine sorted in the first season.

At the end of 1961 Jack Brabham left
the team to build his own cars and Bruce
McLaren took over as first driver. With a
lighter car and a new six speed gearbox in
1962 McLaren managed to come third in
the World Championship. More modifi-
cations followed but without great success;
1959 remained the great Cooper year.

ROVER-BRM TURBO *(centre)*
JET 1 was the first gas turbine saloon car,
produced experimentally by Britain's
Rover car company in 1950. It set the
world's first record for a turbo-engined
car with a flying kilometre at 151.965
m.p.h.

In 1963 came OO, pictured here, a
racing car with the Rover turbine engine,
developed to give 150 b.h.p. at
approaching 40,000 r.p.m., and final
drive by BRM. It was allowed to run in
the Le Mans 24 hours race, though not as
a competitor, and was driven by Graham
Hill and Richie Ginther, who had to
master new techniques to cope with the

engine, which meant cornering with the
power on. They averaged 108 m.p.h.
compared to 118 m.p.h. by the winning
Ferrari and would, in fact, have come
seventh if the car's entry had been
accepted.

Another car was permitted to take
part in the race in 1965 but the engine
overheated and speed was reduced; it was
placed tenth.

RENAULT 'ETOILE FILANTE'
(bottom) An experimental light car, the
Renault 'Shooting Star' pushed the
record for gas turbine machines to 191.2
m.p.h. in 1956. Driven by J. Hébert over

a one-mile course from a flying start, it smashed the record of the pioneering Rover turbo car, but it was never raced.

FERRARI 1.5 FORMULA 1 *(top)*
Ferrari were easily the best prepared team at the start of the 1.5 litre Formula One in 1961; they had been busy while British manufacturers had been waging a fruitless battle to stave off the small-engined formula. And so Ferrari, undistinguished in the dying years of the 2.5 formula, came back with a vengeance.

The Ferrari 156, with its distinctive nostrilled nose, had a 1,476 c.c. V6 engine giving 190 b.h.p. at 9,500 r.p.m.

and the only man who could beat it was Stirling Moss, in Rob Walker's privately entered and outclassed Lotus. The Ferrari drivers Wolfgang von Trips, Giancarlo Baghetti and Phil Hill, won five grandes épreuves and two other Grands Prix.

Von Trips, the first German to win a Grand Prix since 1939, was in line for the World Championship when he met his death at Monza in the Italian Grand Prix and Phil Hill became the first American to win the title.

ALPINE A220 *(bottom)* The glass-fibre body of the Alpine prototype sports car made in Dieppe was so

aerodynamically efficient in styling that it offset to a large extent the comparatively low power from the Renault engine developed by Amédée Gordini.

This was originally a four-cylinder 1,005 c.c. unit developing 105 b.h.p. at 8,500 r.p.m. but 1.3 and 1.5 litre units were among others used with the multi-tubular spaceframe, which was designed by Britain's Len Terry. The picture shows the A220 with an eight-cylinder 2,986 c.c. engine, which was introduced in 1968.

Between 1964 and 1968 these little cars scored a number of placings and class awards in the Le Mans 24 hours race.

PORSCHE 904 GT *(top left)* Porsche contributed to Le Mans history in 1964 when a 2 litre 904 (also known as a Carrera GTS) became the first car to lap the 8.36 mile circuit in under four minutes.

The 904, introduced to racing at the end of 1963, was originally a prototype but was homologated as a GT car (meaning that more than 100 were produced). The first Porsche to be offered to customers with the engine sited behind the driver, it had a horizontally-opposed four-cylinder air-cooled engine which gave 180 b.h.p. at 7,000 r.p.m. and took a number of class awards.

FERRARI SPORTS *(centre left)* From 1960 to 1965 Ferrari were all-powerful in the Le Mans 24 hours race. The cars took first and second places in 1960; first, second and third as well in the next four years.

By 1964, the year of this picture, all Ferrari competition cars were rear-engined (though the forward position was retained for road-going cars). Ferrari 3.3 litre 275P cars and 4 litre 330P cars shared the honours at Le Mans that year, first place going to the 275P of Jean Guichet and Nino Vaccarella at 121.5 m.p.h. But the shadow of Ford was looming over them by then.

LOTUS 30 SPORTS *(bottom left)* The Lotus 30 mounted a 4,727 c.c. 350 b.h.p. Ford V8 engine at the rear of a glass fibre body. It made its first appearance in 1964 and Jim Clark won with it at Silverstone and Goodwood, but it was not a great success.

LOLA T70 SPORTS *(right)* After helping to deliver Ford's GT40 baby, Eric Broadley returned to his works at Slough to create more cars bearing the Lola badge. One of the first was the T70 sports car.

The Mark Two version, introduced in 1966, used a Chevrolet 4,990 c.c. V8 engine producing 430 b.h.p. at 6,000 r.p.m. (though an Aston Martin engine was also used). Driven by John Surtees, Denny Hulme, Frank Gardner, Chris Craft and many others, this car won sports car races all over the world.

COBRA *(top left)* Take a 4.2 litre American Ford engine and install it in an English AC Ace chassis. Result: one of the most potent sports cars ever created, the brainchild of American driver Carroll Shelby. He began producing and racing it in 1962.

Later the power was upped considerably. There were Cobras with 4.7 litre engines giving 350 b.h.p. at 7,000 r.p.m. and 6.9 litre engines giving a massive 490 b.h.p.

In Europe a Cobra won the GT category at Le Mans in 1964, while the Sports Car Club of America Formula A was dominated by the marque. Production ceased in 1967.

FORD GT40 *(centre left)* In the early 1960s Henry Ford II decided to develop a car to win the classic Le Mans 24 hours race, dominated since 1960 by Ferrari.

The Ford challenger was evolved by Eric Broadley, the man who had created the Lola, and was built in Britain by Ford Advanced Vehicles. It was called the GT40 because it stood only 40 inches high, with a 4.2 litre engine giving 350 b.h.p. at 7,200 r.p.m. sited in the midway position.

The car was completed in time for the 1964 race, but it failed. In 1965 it was fitted with a 4.7 litre engine giving 390 b.h.p. at 7,000 r.p.m. Six cars were entered for Le Mans, but all retired.

In 1966 came the Mark Two with a 6,997 c.c. engine giving 500 b.h.p. at 6,400 r.p.m. and automatic transmission, and Fords finished first, second and third, the winning team being Bruce McLaren and Chris Amon at 125.38 m.p.h.

Ford then dominated Le Mans, winning again in 1967, 1968 and 1969, by which time they had proved their point and the project was ended.

MERLYN FORMULA FORD *(bottom left)* Formula Ford was evolved in Britain in 1967 to allow young drivers to race single-seaters at low cost. The formula calls for a 1600 c.c. Ford Cortina crossflow production engine with only limited tuning, and road tyres as opposed to racing ones.

The Merlyn, designed by Chris Maskery and Selwyn Hayward, and built by Colchester Racing, soon became the top car in the formula. Australian Tim Schenken entered Formula One racing after being Formula Ford champion in a Merlyn in 1968 and 1969.

EAGLE 3 litre FORMULA 1 *(top right)* American Dan Gurney inspired it and drove it, but the Eagle Formula One car was made in England, hence 'Anglo-American Racers', the name that Gurney gave his team.

The Eagle had a chassis by former Lotus designer Len Terry and a 2,997 c.c. V12 engine giving 420 b.h.p. at 10,000 r.p.m. by former Jaguar cylinder-head expert Harold Weslake. Gurney drove it first in the Italian Grand Prix of 1966, then in 1967 the New Yorker won the Race of Champions at Brands Hatch and the Belgian Grand Prix at Spa.

But Gurney was soon concentrating on producing a different kind of Eagle to win the big-money Indianapolis 500. He was successful in that ambition, Bobby Unser driving an Eagle to victory in the 1968 race, but Gurney could not devote the same attention to the Formula One cars and they were withdrawn at the end of the season.

BRABHAM-REPCO 3 litre FORMULA 1
(bottom right) When the 3 litre Formula One began in 1966 most teams were developing sophisticated V12 engines, but Jack Brabham gambled on simplicity and cheapness. He used an Australian Repco engine of 2,996 c.c., based on a well-tried General Motors unit. It gave some 330 b.h.p. at 8,800 r.p.m., which made it gutless compared to its rivals, but Brabham had been right; what it lacked in power it made up for in reliability. And the space-frame body designed by Ron Tauranac was light and responsive.

In 1966 Brabham won his third World Championship in it and became the first driver to take the title in a car of his own construction. The following year his team mate, New Zealander Denny Hulme, won the title with Brabham runner-up. But by that time Brabham knew that the Repco had had its day and in 1969 he switched to the ubiquitous Ford-Cosworth engine used by the majority of his rivals.

McLAREN 3 litre FORMULA 1
(previous page) Bruce McLaren died in June 1970 while testing a Can-Am car at Goodwood. His fellow-countryman Denny Hulme took over as leader of the McLaren team and, despite burned hands suffered in practice for the Indianapolis 500, managed to come fourth in the Drivers' World Championship that year.

FERRARI 3 litre FORMULA 1 *(top left)*
The first full 3 litre Grand Prix car of 1966 was the Ferrari V12. Initially it had two valves per cylinder, later three valves per cylinder, and the light alloy engine of 2,985 c.c. developed 436 b.h.p. at 11,000 r.p.m.
New Zealander Chris Amon (seen in the picture) was its chief driver but the car's failures became notorious. He left Ferrari at the end of 1969 to join March.

VOLKSWAGEN FORMULA VEE
(centre left) Formula Vee originated in the United States in 1963 with the same object as Formula Ford. It requires single-seat cars built from standard Volkswagen parts, including the 1300 c.c. engine, clutch, gearbox and suspension. Many small firms have produced these cars and Helmut Marko is one top driver who graduated from Formula Vee.
In 1970 Super Vee was introduced to cater for cars with 1600 c.c. engines.

HONDA 3 litre FORMULA 1 *(bottom left)* Honda embarked on the 3 litre formula in 1966 with a bulky 2,992 c.c. V12 engine developing 420 b.h.p. at 9,500 r.p.m. John Surtees became the chief driver in 1967 and won the Italian Grand Prix at Monza but little else.
In 1968 Honda introduced a light-weight air-cooled V8 engine of 2,987 c.c. giving 430 b.h.p. at 10,500 r.p.m. Jo Schlesser of France drove it at Rouen, but crashed in the rain and died in flames. Honda withdrew from racing at the end of the year and Surtees went to BRM.

COOPER-MASERATI 3 litre FORMULA 1 *(right)* Cooper's star had waned after the Formula One championship years of 1959 and 1960. In 1965 the firm became part of the Chipstead Motors group, which imported foreign cars, and as a result, arrangements were made to utilize a 2,989 c.c. Maserati V12 engine for the 1966 3 litre Grand Prix formula. This engine gave some 350 b.h.p. at 9,500 r.p.m. in a monocoque body – the first Cooper utilized, which was designed by Tony Robinson.
John Surtees, Jochen Rindt and Pedro Rodriguez were the drivers, but though the car was reliable it was heavy and slow, and in 1967 a new Maserati engine with three valves per cylinder was adopted. This gave more power, and Rodriguez won the South African Grand Prix, but reliability suffered. In 1968 Cooper switched to a BRM V12 engine, but the car was still uncompetitive and the name faded quietly from the racing scene.

LOTUS-FORD FORMULA 3 *(top left)*
Formula Three is the traditional 'nursery' for the Formula One stars of the future. It began after the war with 500 c.c. engined midgets but from 1964 to 1970 the formula called for 1 litre engines using production cylinder blocks and heads to keep down cost and performance. In practice, all British cars used four-cylinder 105E Ford units of 997 c.c., giving around 120 b.h.p. at 10,000 r.p.m.

Morris Nunn was a works driver of the Lotus model, later producing his own Formula Three car, the Ensign.

BRABHAM-FORD FORMULA 3
(bottom left) Since 1971 Formula Three has allowed production units of up to 1600 c.c., which has meant a Ford twin-cam motor for most competitors. But additional restrictions cut the power to some 105 b.h.p.

Colin Vandervell, son of the Vanwall creator, was outstanding with a Brabham car, the most consistently successful marque in Formula Three for several years.

MARCH 701 *(top right)* To create a completely new Formula One contender and to have it outnumbering all other makes on the starting grid a few months later was the formidable achievement of Max Mosley, Robin Herd, Alan Rees and their associates at the start of the 1970 season. From their works at Bicester (Oxford) came cars for their own works team and many private entrants, among them Ken Tyrrell, who bought the car pictured for 1969 World Champion Jackie Stewart to drive. The car had a monocoque body, a Cosworth-Ford V8 engine and Hewland five-speed gearbox.

The first March victory was scored by Stewart in the Race of Champions at Brands Hatch and he went on to win the Spanish Grand Prix, but by mid-season the Lotus 72 and the Ferrari had been sorted and the March appeared to have weight and handling problems. For 1971 there came the March 711 with a completely new body.

MATRA-SIMCA 3 litre FORMULA 1
(bottom right) Following the merger of the French firms of Matra and Simca, the Matra Formula One team reverted in 1970 to using a developed form of the V12 engine which they had first used in 1968. The car's chassis was functional and the roadholding was good but the engine was low in the league for power at first.

A slow puncture robbed Jean-Pierre Beltoise of victory in the French Grand Prix and the team could only secure a trio of third placings to end equal sixth with BRM in the Constructors' Championship.

ALPINE-RENAULT FORMULA 3 *(top left)* France's Alpine company, long associated with Renault, inevitably use the Renault engine which is the only one to rival Ford power. Alpine drivers Alain Serpaggi and Michel Leclerc were the French champions in 1971.

LOTUS-FORD FORMULA 2 *(centre left)* Formula Two is motor racing's second division, but it has seldom been second rate in quality. In 1964, when Formula One engines were limited to 1.5 litres, Formula Two cars were restricted to 1 litre; the Lotus-Ford 32 was driven by Jim Clark to four victories that year.

SURTEES-FORD FORMULA 2 *(bottom left)* In 1972, after five years of racing under a 1,600 c.c. limit, Formula Two was changed to allow engines of up to 2 litres. One of the first of the new cars was the Surtees TS10 which used a Ford engine, like virtually all its rivals. It was driven with distinction by Mike Hailwood.

PORSCHE 917 SPORTS *(top right)* Porsche were estimated to have spent £2 millions on the development of this car, the greatest long distance racer of the seventies. Introduced in 1969, it was champion sports car of that year and of 1970 and 1971, after which the 5 litre sports car formula with its astronomically rising costs was replaced by a 3 litre formula.

The 4,907 c.c. 12 cylinder Porsche engine, air-cooled by a fan, gave 600 b.h.p. at 8,400 r.p.m. and the car was capable of nearly 240 m.p.h. Within its aluminium spaceframe covered by glass fibre bodywork it could carry 26.5 gallons of fuel and it burned a gallon every 5.8 miles at Le Mans in 1971 when Pedro Rodriguez set a lap record speed of 151.81 m.p.h.

The race was won however by another 917 driven by Helmut Marko and Gijs van Lennep at an average of 138.1 m.p.h. over 3,315 miles. Inevitably it was the swan song of this reliable car at Le Mans.

FERRARI 312 SPORTS *(bottom right)* Ferrari's sports car of the seventies, built to the 3 litre limit, was designed by Mauro Forghieri and Giacomo Caliri and used a tubular spaceframe reinforced with riveted sheet aluminium, and a 12 cylinder Ferrari engine of 2,991 c.c. giving more than 450 b.h.p.

Jacky Ickx and Clay Regazzoni were among those who drove it.

McLAREN-CHEVROLET F5000 *(top left)* Designed to produce spectacular single-seat racing at lower cost than Grand Prix cars, Formula 5000 was introduced to Britain in 1969, patterned on the American Formula A, and using mass-produced engines of up to 5 litres. Nearly all the cars have been powered by 4,992 c.c. Chevrolet V8s, and the three F5000 cars shown in this book use them.

The McLaren M10B was developed by Jo Marquandt from a design by Robin Herd and marketed at £4,850 without the engine. One was raced with outstanding success by Peter Gethin in the first two years of the formula and later by Graham McRae.

LOLA-CHEVROLET F5000 *(centre left)* When Australian Frank Gardner began driving a Lola in F5000 races he soon developed ideas about improving it. He had the wheelbase lengthened by nine inches and the weight lowered by 100 lb. The result was the T300 and in it he became F5000 champion in 1971.

SURTEES-CHEVROLET F5000 *(bottom left)* Ex-world champion on two wheels and four, John Surtees made his debut as a manufacturer with a F5000 car in 1969 and it was the most successful car of the first year. The TS8 was driven in 1971 with considerable success by another ex-motorcycle champion, Mike Hailwood.

SEVENTIES

McLAREN M16B INDIANAPOLIS

(previous page) Mark Donohue had led the 1971 Indianapolis race for 66 laps and was then forced to drop out. In 1972 he did not take the lead until lap 188, with only 12 left to go. And then he won at a new record speed of 163.465 m.p.h. and collected some 218,000 dollars in prize money.

MARTINI-TECNO FORMULA 1 *(top left)*

Brothers Luciano and Gianfranco Pederzani began by making karts in 1962. They progressed via Formula Four, Three and Two, arriving in Formula One in 1972.

The Bologna brothers' Formula One car, backed by an Italian aperitif firm, was virtually the only spaceframe car on the circuits; it was also shorter than most. The Tecno 12-cylinder 2,997 c.c. engine gave 440 b.h.p. at 12,000 r.p.m. and the cars were driven by Nanni Galli and Derek Bell, but appearances were too rare in 1972 to assess its potential.

MARCH-FORD 721 FORMULA 1

(centre left) The 1972 March had a full monocoque chassis by Robin Herd and a body by Frank Costin that featured water radiators on either side of the cockpit. It was another of the many that used the Ford V8 engine.

At the wheel in the picture is Mike Beuttler, Cairo-born Englishman whose entries were backed by a consortium of four stockbrokers.

YARDLEY McLAREN-FORD FORMULA 1 *(bottom left)*

Designed by Ralph Bellamy, the McLaren M19 of 1972 was also a full monocoque using the Ford V8 engine. It is driven here by American Peter Revson.

JOHN PLAYER SPECIAL FORD *(top right)*

This was the name used in 1972 for what had previously been known as the Lotus-Ford. Its V8 engine was now giving up to 450 b.h.p. at 11,000 r.p.m. and its reliability had been improved and it was a triumphant year for Colin Chapman's team after some time in the doldrums.

Emerson Fittipaldi, sixth in the World Championship for the team in 1971, won the Italian Grand Prix at Monza in September at 131.61 m.p.h. and clinched the Championship title before the season was complete.

The 25-year-old Brazilian who had travelled to England in 1969 with just enough money to buy a Formula Ford, became the youngest champion ever.

FERRARI 312 FORMULA 1 *(bottom right)*

Italy's other contender in Formula One in 1972 was the Ferrari with its flat-12 engine of 2,998 c.c. and 470 b.h.p. Designed by Mauro Forghieri, it was a 'false monocoque' with a spaceframe reinforced by riveted sheet aluminium.

MARLBORO-BRM FORMULA 1 *(top)*

Another new car in 1972 was the BRM P180 driven by jockey's son Peter Gethin. He had joined BRM from McLaren in mid-1971 after the death of Pedro Rodriguez and gave the team victory in the 1971 Italian Grand Prix at Monza by a distance of 24 inches.

The P180 was designed by Tony Southgate, a semi-monocoque with a tubular rear subframe and two radiators at the back. Its BRM V12 engine of 2,999 c.c. gave 440 b.h.p. at 10,750 r.p.m.

TYRRELL-FORD FORMULA 1

(bottom) Jackie Stewart won the World Championship in 1971 in a Tyrrell-Ford with almost twice as many points as his nearest rival, Ronnie Peterson in a March-Ford.

For 1972 he had a new car, created by Derek Gardner, who has also done design work on rockets and jet aircraft. A semi-monocoque, it had a radically new aerodynamic shape and for the first time the rear-mounted Ford V8 3 litre engine was almost totally enclosed.

Biggest change in the car mechanically was that the front disc brakes were moved inboard. The car had a theoretical top speed of over 190 m.p.h.

SURTEES-FORD FORMULA 1 *(top left)* 'Big John' Surtees designed his own full monocoque car for 1972, using the Ford V8 engine. It is driven here by Australian Tim Schenken.

BRABHAM-FORD FORMULA 1 *(centre left)* Ron Tauranac designed the Brabham BT34 with its distinctive 'lobster claw' front, a full monocoque car using the Ford V8 engine. It is seen driven by Wilson Fittipaldi, younger brother of Emerson.

CHAPARRAL CAN-AM *(bottom left)* Popularly known as 'the Hoover car', the Chaparral 2J used the principle of a hovercraft in reverse. A 45 b.h.p. two-cylinder two-stroke engine drove two rear-facing fans which, with the aid of a skirt, exerted a suction effect to hold the car on the ground when cornering fast.

Texan Jim Hall, the Chaparral chief, used the sucker device, designed by Don Gates, in a car with a 7.6 litre engine in the Can-Am series of 1970. Jackie Stewart made the fastest lap at Watkins Glen in the USA in the car in July, but it failed to finish in any race and by the end of the year the gimmick had been banned by the FIA.

MARCH 707 CAN-AM *(top right)* The Canadian-American Challenge Cup series, which began in 1966, features some of the fastest cars in the world, for though they must have two-seater bodies, they are built purely for racing and engine size is unlimited. In practice, this means the use of big Chevrolet V8 engines.

In 1970 came the wedge-shaped March 707, driven by Helmut Kelleners. It was bigger than most Can-Am cars, with a 96-inch wheelbase, and used a 7.6 litre Chevrolet engine, but it could not equal the McLaren.

McLAREN-CHEVROLET CAN-AM *(bottom right)* McLaren cars dominated the Can-Am series from its inception. In 1969 two McLarens with 6,997 c.c. Chevrolet V8 engines developing over 600 b.h.p. were driven by Bruce himself and his fellow New Zealander Denny Hulme to 11 victories in 11 races and they also took eight second placings.

The whole racing world was shocked when Bruce McLaren died while testing a new Can-Am car at Goodwood the following year. But the firm has continued and in 1971 Peter Revson (pictured here) became the first American to win a Can-Am series, driving a McLaren M8F of some 740 b.h.p.

LOTUS Mark 56 INDIANAPOLIS *(top)*
America's banked Indianapolis speedway has its own special requirements in the way of cars. The wedge-shaped Lotus Mark 56, created to compete in the Indianapolis 500 mile race of 1968, was powered by a Pratt and Whitney gas turbine motor and equipped with Ferguson four-wheel drive.

Taking the place of Jim Clark, who had been killed at Hockenheim, Croydon driver Mike Spence set the second fastest lap recorded on the brick track in practice at 169.5 m.p.h. But in a later practice session he crashed while lapping at 163 m.p.h., and died in hospital.

EAGLE-OFFENHAUSER INDIANAPOLIS *(bottom)* Bobby Unser, winner of the Indianapolis 500 race in 1968, set a new Indy lap record of 196.678 m.p.h. and averaged 195.940 m.p.h. in his Eagle when qualifying for the 1972 race.

The four-cylinder Drake-Offenhauser turbo-charged engine was giving more than 900 b.h.p. and advantage had been taken of new, more permissive regulations, to set the car's wings higher and further back. In the race Unser led until the thirty-first lap, when the distributor failed.